THE
HEART
OF SELLING

JACQUI SAKOWSKI

♥

Madison, Wisconsin
www.goblinfernpress.com

Copyright © 2004 By Jacqui Sakowski/Sakowski Consulting, LLC.

All rights reserved. No part of this book may be used or reproduced in any manner whatsoever without written permission from the publisher and the author, except in the case of brief quotations embodied in critical articles and reviews.

For information, please address Goblin Fern Press, Inc., 3809 Mineral Point Road, Madison, WI 53705. www.goblinfernpress.com or toll-free: 888-670-BOOK (2665).

Goblin Fern Press books may be purchased for educational, business or sales promotional use. Quantity discounts available.

ISBN: 1-59598-004-0

Cover design: Melissa Carlson, Melissa Carlson Creative
Photography: Shannon McMahan Designer Portraits
Book design and typesetting: Kristin Girvin Redman

Printed in the United States of America

First Edition

Mary Kay,

With the quality of your Heart you are sure to prosper!

Jeeger

For Robert
whose love empowers me
to be the best I can be
in all aspects of my life.

Contents

INTRODUCTION ix

HONOR 1
   Know your clients 3
   Be prepared 8
   Know what you sell 10
   Know your organization 12
   Share your resources 14

ENTHUSIASM 23
   Source of enthusiasm 24
   Maintaining enthusiasm 27
   Enthusiasm for the products 29
   Fascination 32

ACCOUNTABILITY 41
   Training 45
   Fit to work 46
   Knowledge of your organization 49
   Knowledge about your clients 52
   Knowledge of your industry 54
   Knowledge—closing the deal 56
   Knowledge—understanding 57

RESOLVE 67
   Attracting new clients 70
   Commit to the task 73
   Persevere to the end 75
   Imagination and creativity 78

TRUST 89
Integrity. 91
The truth, the whole truth, and nothing but the truth 95
Treat customers fairly 97
Say what you do and do what you say 100
Supporters. 103

EPILOGUE 113

HONOR ROLL 117

RESOURCES 121

ABOUT THE AUTHOR 123

INTRODUCTION

As sales professionals, we are facing a whole new set of dynamics as we do business in the twenty-first century.

Consumers are becoming much more values-oriented and making powerful emotional connections to the products and services they buy. They wish to leave a meaningful legacy in their wake. They seek more substance and purpose in their lives. In their personal lives, they seek fulfilling relationships inside and outside of their families. They look for life-affirming volunteer opportunities and they read books that help them better understand who they are. In their professional lives, they seek to work in jobs and companies that serve a greater good than simply producing financial rewards and investor returns. They look for evidence of corporate responsibility and accountability. They seek a community of colleagues who share their most precious values. They wish to work with vendors who understand their vision and are committed to helping them reach their goals.

"The shift in thinking is from asking how we can motivate consumers to buy our product to asking instead how we can touch our consumers' lives. And I mean asking that question with absolute sincerity and passion." writes Marc Gobé, author of *Citizen Brand*. "Tapping emotions is not top-of-mind yet in all consumer decisions," he says. "But this is a long-lasting trend, toward a new way of consumer thinking."

As sales professionals, we are facing a whole new set of dynamics as we do business in the twenty-first century.

We need to develop a personal brand. We need to show clients and prospective clients that our personal brand respects and shares their values; that we are concerned about more than simply selling more products and services and generating more profits. We need to show them that our heart is as engaged as our head when we do business.

Probably the biggest challenge sales professionals face is the mistrust of buyers. Far too many consumers have experienced poor sales practices and are quite naturally wary of being duped again. Throughout the pages of this book, you will learn how to show your clients your integrity, your reliability and your commitment. You will learn how to show them that your heart is as engaged as your head.

When you visit the book store, you will find many books on selling; most of them focus primarily on the sales process. They describe well-practiced sales processes that have proven successful over time for their authors. And I absolutely support the fundamental messages that they share. "Process equals productivity" and "It's all about the relationship."

Selling, like almost every other aspect of business, is a process. You begin the process by identifying prospective customers for your product or service. You work through your sales process and eventually you get an audience with them. Now that you have your chance, how do you show your prospects that your heart is as engaged as your head? How do you help them make an emotional connection to you, your products, your services and your brand? How do you convince your existing clients that the grass really is greenest on your side of the fence? How do you build their loyalty so they see no need to look elsewhere? How do you build the unbreakable bond that is at the core of a *great sales relationship?*

You create that bond by showing your prospects and clients that you are a sales professional from whom they will enjoy many benefits beyond simply doing business... by putting your HEART into it!

This book is not about sales process. This book is about how to show your clients and associates that you are a sales professional with whom they will wish to do business because of the many benefits you bring them.

Being a sales professional that others wish to do business with is as important to your success as any process. Being a sales professional that others wish to do business with makes it easier to get in front of prospective clients. It makes it easier to convert prospects into clients. Being a sales professional who others wish to do business with enables you to create a bond between you and your clients that is almost impossible for your competitors to break. It's the difference between building a sales relationship and building a ***great sales relationship.***

The HEART of Selling discusses the five elements, which I believe empower ***great sales relationships***—Honor, Enthusiasm, Accountability, Resolve and Trust. It discusses ways to show clients and prospects that you are a sales professional with whom they can make an emotional connection.

The ideas discussed here are applicable to all sales environments. Whether you're working in a small company or a major corporation. Whether you're looking to generate a seven-figure income or your goals are less ambitious. Whether you're a sole proprietor working in a home-based business or a hi-tech entrepreneur looking to change the world. The foundation of your sales success will be the strength of the relationships you build with clients and business associates. While every industry may have its own characteristics, the fundamentals of building a ***great sales relationship*** are the same because relationships are built between people.

Companies are built by people. Products are built by people. Services are delivered by people. Products and services are used by people. As sales professionals, we need to focus on the people first. When the people are with us, we can apply our process.

As you read the five sections of the book, you will find some repeating themes. This book is about taking a holistic approach; it's about nurturing your client relationships. Applying just one or two of the elements will not produce the same outcomes as using them all in combination. They are each a part of another and cannot successfully be divided.

By putting HEART into every sales relationship, you will earn the trust and confidence of your clients, you will enjoy improved sales results and you will have a lot more fun! Enjoy it.

Jacqui

HONOR

respect • admiration • reverence

Honor is a nice word. It sounds like something good. It conjures up long-forgotten times of knights in shining armor who are always doing the right thing for others and for themselves. It conjures up thoughts of fairness, honesty, respectability, morality and ethics. It reminds us of the Honor Roll at school, when we learned that there was more to being a great student than simply getting great grades.

♥

Honor is a word we hear far too seldom in business these days and yet it embraces the very essence of ***great sales relationships***. Honor means behaving ethically when we deliver on the agreements and contracts we make. It means respecting our clients, our colleagues, our vendors and, most importantly, ourselves. It means abiding by the regulations that govern our industry and working within the laws society has created to define good business practices.

To most of us, these are simply the right things to do. We don't need to think about them. In fact, the only time we may think about them is when we learn of folks who are not exhibiting appropriate behavior!

When we do think about honor, though, we think of it in regard to honoring our clients, our colleagues, our vendors and our associates. We think about presenting them with a reward in exchange for an accomplishment. We think about bestowing a title such as "Dealer of the Year" to our top client. We induct our top seller into "The President's Club" or we nominate an "Employee of the Month," for exceptional effort throughout the period.

We envision paying tribute to these special few in an elegant setting acknowledging their efforts with an award or a plaque. They win some extraordinary prize for some extra special effort. They stand up at the annual banquet, sales conference or monthly staff meeting. They are showered with praise and publicity and a wonderful few moments are had by all. They experience a tremendous sense of appreciation. They remind themselves how hard they worked to earn the moment and they quite rightly take pride in knowing they did well. It's a good feeling! A very good feeling!

While it is exciting and uplifting to present awards to honor clients, colleagues, vendors and associates in recognition of their special accomplishments from time to time—perhaps monthly or annually—it is imperative that we honor their everyday contributions as well. After all, more success is built by ordinary actions than extraordinary ones!

As sales professionals, we must honor the people who contribute to our success every day—our clients and customers, our vendors and our co-workers—by the way we interact with them. This does not mean showering them with awards and gifts, but rather, with skill and knowledge, commitment and honesty, fairness and integrity, courtesy and respect.

Know your clients

As a first-time home owner in 1981, I did not feel honored by my insurance agent when he came to call on me one evening. I had owned the house for about a month and had been excitedly decorating and stamping my identity all over it, so I was thrilled when he congratulated me on the difference I'd made since his previous visit. When he then called me by the wrong name and I told him he that he had done so, he asked the address. When I told him, "34 Ingleby Road," he replied, "Oops, wrong house." and left without apology! To this day, I doubt the sincerity of his comments about my decorating.

One very important way we honor our clients is to make the effort to really get to know them. To understand what makes them tick. Target marketing practices compel us to define our clients in some detail. We develop tools to analyze an array of demographic and psychographic data to develop a profile of customers most likely to buy our products. We can maximize our resources by focusing all our attention on winning business from organizations or individuals who fit this profile. But don't make the mistake of assuming that people who fit the profile all think and act the same way for the same reasons. They don't. They simply belong to a group that has a greater propensity to buy what we sell.

Personalizing your sales relationships, by taking the time to really get to know and understand your clients, helps to build the deep and unbreakable bond of trust that is the foundation of every *great sales relationship.*

When we first meet a prospective client, we may be hesitant to delve too deeply into intimate areas of their business. We may be cautious about appearing insensitive to the more private aspects of their lives. Nevertheless, we need to get as close as possible to these areas if we are to partner with them in identifying solutions to the challenges they face.

Today, we are able to obtain an extraordinary amount of information about prospective corporate clients before we ever make contact with them. The World Wide Web gives us access to detailed descriptions of product and service offerings; company and organizational structures; markets served; history, vision, mission and goals. We can find the names of key personnel and often even details of our client's customers.

While it may be more difficult to learn about individual consumers and smaller corporations before you meet, it is amazing how much information is available via web searches. Do a web search on your own name, your own company and your own industry. You will most likely be quite surprised by what you find. A web search on my name brought up most of my professional affiliations, my company, other members of my U.S.-based family and many of the speaking and teaching events I have undertaken.

There really is very little reason not to know plenty about our clients. By the time we make an initial approach to a prospective client we should have a good sense of whom we are addressing. With such thorough preparation, we can quickly display our commitment to a prospective client, the very first time we meet, by showing the investment we have already made in learning about them and their business. There should be no doubt that we are serious about wishing to do business with this client in particular. Not with companies like theirs or companies in their community, but very specifically with them. This is personal, so dig deep!

During our research, what we learned from their web site and other publicly-posted information is what the company would like its public to know. What we learned was written with prospective customers in mind, not necessarily prospective vendors.

To be effective sales professionals, ones who honor their clients and customers, we need to learn what is actually going on inside the business, out of sight of customers and competitors. What are the priorities and the challenges the company or organization faces as it strives to achieve its goals and to live up to its vision and mission? Where is the connection to us? To our company and to our vision, mission and goals? What do we share in common? How do we differ?

In every meeting and conversation, make a major effort to learn more from your clients than simply about the area of their life or business that specifically affects you. You need more than an order from your interactions. You need to build a long-term relationship, which provides regular benefits to all the parties involved. Think bigger than today's order: think bigger than this week's, this month's or even this year's sales goal. Think about building a relationship, which will bring benefit to your client and you over a lifetime.

When I sit down with a company for the first time, I explain to the person I am meeting that I have a process. That I like to learn about his or her business in general before getting into the specific issue that generated the meeting. I have between twenty and thirty background questions about the business that I wish to ask before I ask about the product or service I am there to sell. It is through these broader business questions that I learn the context in which my product or service could be used. It is how I uncover the synergy between our two organizations. It is where I identify the connections between our vision, mission and goals.

Many times I am told, "I've never met anyone who asked so many questions." I reply, quite sincerely, "Unless I learn everything I can about your business, I won't know if what I provide can be of benefit to you." I display my genuine interest in what makes this company or person unique and in doing so, I differentiate myself from other sales professionals. I make it personal, I dig deep and my questions enable me to gain powerful insights into the company. Insights that my competitors generally don't get!

Always assume you are competing for the client's business against someone else who offers at least as good a solution as you do, possibly better. If you have all the available information that the client can provide and more information than your competitors, you are in the best position to craft an ideal solution that will meet your client's needs. The more you know about what the client wishes to accomplish, the more support you can offer. If you have more information than your competitors, you are more likely to win a bigger share of the business.

Every time you meet with a client or prospect, your goal should be two-fold: First, to determine whether or not your product or service will be of benefit to the prospect and second, to build a ***great sales relationship*** with an unbreakable bond. The more you learn, the more information you have, the easier it will be to accomplish both goals.

Be prepared

We honor our clients by respecting the time they commit to us by preparing ourselves well for any and every interaction.

We should always assume that our client's time is as scarce and as precious as our own. Therefore we must respect the time our clients share with us by using it productively. How do we do this? By arriving at our meetings on time, properly prepared to do business. By arriving at our meetings with all the information, tools, samples and paperwork we need to complete our agenda.

Customers start to develop trust in a sales professional when they see that person making a real investment in building the relationship, when they see the sales professional striving to provide real and lasting value to their company or organization. One way clients recognize this investment is by how well prepared the sales professional is in all their interactions.

Sales professionals have a reputation for being self-centered. For being focused on their own goals, their own products and their own needs in the relationship.

When you sit down with your client and open the meeting by reminding her why the meeting is taking place, you prove that you have a purpose for being there. When you share the research you have undertaken to acquaint yourself with her business or industry, you indicate your commitment to providing individual service. When you summarize the issues she has indicated need to be discussed and show that you have brought information and answers to address those issues, you reveal that you have been investing resources in serving her, even though no business has yet been transacted.

By focusing on the client's agenda and using her time productively, you have already differentiated yourself from most of the sales professionals with whom you are competing for her business. You have honored your prospect's time and made the best use of your own by preparing well for the meeting.

Even when your sales environment does not lend itself to formal business meetings, you can demonstrate your commitment to honoring your clients by being well prepared to serve them. For example, store displays are changed regularly to keep them looking fresh and interesting, so make the effort to know where everything is in the showroom's current layout. Be familiar with current inventory. Be able to provide accurate information immediately when asked questions by customers. Keep up to date with lead times, so you know when new inventory will arrive. Be prepared and be a resource to even the most casual customers and they will be honored by that.

Know what you sell

As sales professionals, we can take it for granted that we should always be well prepared for meetings. Being properly prepared to do business extends well beyond simply turning up to a meeting with all the materials and information you need to answer the questions, propose a solution and close a sale! It's much more than knowing the location of goods in the store. Being properly prepared to do business is also about knowledge and expertise.

Our clients deserve the very best of us, at all times. They should have confidence that we have all the knowledge and expertise necessary to guide them in making high-quality, strategic decisions that will take them nearer to their goals.

It is obvious to anyone that sales professionals should know their products or services inside and out. If they don't, how can they craft the best possible solution or discuss the available options confidently?

Knowing your products inside and out means knowing much more than which buttons to push to make them work. Knowing your services inside and out means knowing much more than what actions will be performed by you or your colleagues.

Knowing your products and or services means understanding why they were developed in the first place. Where did the ideas come from? Did you or your company develop the idea from scratch? Who has the patent if one exists? Where did your products or services come from and where are they going? You should understand the history of your products or services, of your company and of your industry. You should know how your products or services differ from those of your competitors. You should be aware of future possibilities and industry and market trends.

The more knowledgeable you are about your products and services, the easier it is for buyers to place their trust in you. The more knowledgeable you are the easier it is to build a ***great sales relationship*** with an unbreakable bond.

Know your organization

We honor our clients by ensuring that all their needs in their relationship with our organization are taken care of. To do so, we need to know our organization inside and out. We need to know our organization as thoroughly as we know our products and services.

We need to know the policies, procedures and systems that will enable us to serve our client's every need. If we don't have all the answers, we should know how to get them and from whom. We should be able to provide the names of the people who will solve the problems, not just the names of the departments in which they work.

For example, your client will feel so much more confident that an invoicing error will be fixed when he hears you say, "I'll speak with Wendy Harrison in Accounts Receivable and ask her to adjust that immediately." The fact that you know Wendy's name implies to the client you have a relationship with her and that she will respond to your request for assistance. "I'll ask Dave Webb, the lead design and development engineer, to take a look at this," is so much more powerful than "I'll get Engineering to take a look."

If you're a sole proprietor, you likely designed all your policies and procedures yourself, and you'll take care of everything yourself anyway. But do you know how the carrier service you work with does things? Do you know what will happen if a shipment goes astray? Do you know how your credit card processor will handle an overcharged account? The organizations that supply services to us, which directly affect our client relationships, are an extension of our business. We need to be familiar with their procedures too, so that when we need to get something done, we can be confident of making it happen.

Buyers like to know they are working with sales professionals who can get things accomplished. Show your clients that you have a thorough understanding of how things work in your company. Make them aware of the relationships you have with colleagues throughout your organization. Doing so will build your client's confidence that you can get action when needed.

You must become part of the package they buy. You must be the added value they need to make a decision in your favor. It's not just about the product or service. You may be the only person from your company that the client ever sees. The impression you make may be the only image he or she may ever have of your company or organization. You are the personification of your company or organization!

The fact is: there will always be someone else who can offer a product or service like yours. There will always be someone else striving to take your clients away from you. You may be the only unique part of the package and *no one else can be you!* Differentiate yourself from your competitors by preparing yourself thoroughly to do business. Honor your customers by letting them see how capable you are.

Share your resources

We honor our clients when we pay attention to the wider issues of their business. Once you thoroughly understand your client's business and become an enthusiastic supporter, you can be an advocate for that business among other people in your circle.

You can talk about the business with other companies that may have potential to buy your client's products or services. You can introduce the company to potential vendors or strategic partners. When your clients see you are such an enthusiastic and committed servant of their company, they cannot help but become more loyal to you in return.

> When coaching Lori, the owner of a health claims administration company, I took the liberty of asking some bankers I knew if they would be willing to introduce her to the relevant people in their organizations. A couple of them responded positively. After meeting with one of them, Lori developed a completely new product line, which solved a problem for that bank and offered potential for a significant increase in business for her. I could not have made those introductions if I had not learned enough about her business to know those introductions would be valuable.

Whether or not the introductions you make for your clients develop into powerful relationships, the fact that you make the effort to serve them so completely is a signal to your clients of your total commitment to their business success. You show them that your investment in your relationship with them goes far beyond simply taking their orders and making a profit. By bringing relevant contacts and connections to them, you show your clients you really have taken the time to listen and understand what it is they do in their company and what makes a good customer, vendor or partner for them.

By taking the time out of your already-full schedule to facilitate the introduction, you show the client that you genuinely care about his or her business success. Eventually the client will recognize you and your organization as a necessary adjunct to their business. You become partners.

> I once set up and attended a meeting between the owner of a printing firm and the owner of an advertising specialties firm. One was my client, the other was my vendor. I saw great potential for them to work together as they serve a similar target market. After sitting in the meeting for about half an hour, I left them to their discussion. The strategic partnership I had suggested did not develop, but both recognized and appreciated my effort to help them grow their businesses.

At least once a month, review your contact list to see if there are new connections to be made among the people, companies and organizations that you know. When you learn new information about your clients, vendors and associates, look for connections that may not have occurred to you previously. For example, if you learn that someone you know has developed a new product line or service, look to see if that may benefit others in your circle.

Taking some time to consider how you can help your clients beyond simply supplying them with your products or services is a great way to show them how genuinely committed you are to helping them meet their goals. By accepting your introduction, they demonstrate that you have earned their trust. A referral from a trusted business associate is an increasingly popular mechanism for finding new customers and new resources. The success of organizations such as Business Network International (BNI) is testament to that.

All over the world thousands of chapters of BNI meet weekly. The members are there to build relationships, which result in business by referral. They meet to educate one another about their offerings, so they may speak authoritatively about each others businesses. They use one another's products and services and share their personal experiences with their contacts. Whenever BNI members hear a client or an associate of theirs express a need, which may be met by a fellow chapter member, they introduce the parties to one another.

Referrals are the sole source of new business opportunities for many sales professionals. It takes a good deal of time to get to know new vendors or clients. We have to learn about their background, their values, their products, their pricing, their distribution methods, their advantages and their disadvantages. Trust has to be built between the buyer and the seller. How much faster to a solution then, if we can meet someone who is already known and trusted by someone whose judgment we already respect!

Finding ways to serve your clients through introductions to trustworthy professionals in other fields actually enables you to honor your client and to honor the other professionals in your circle. After all, you would not introduce someone to your client who did not have your respect. You would not introduce someone you were not confident would honor your clients with honesty, integrity, fairness and respect. You would not introduce someone who would be likely to embarrass you and possibly jeopardize your relationship with your client.

♥

How will you honor your clients?

Take the risk of digging deeper to get a more complete picture of your client's needs, wants and desires. Are your questions deep enough?

Some questions to get you started

How did the company begin?

What exactly do you do?

Who is (are) your client(s)?

What problem does your product or service address for your client(s)?

Who are your competitors?

What differentiates you from your competitors?

What are your current business priorities?

What are your current business challenges?

When you sit in your hot tub and dream, what do you envision for the future of your company?

If you lost your biggest client, what impact would that have on your business?

Expertise

Share your extensive knowledge and expertise with your clients, gain their confidence and respect and increase the value of the total package you provide. Be honest with yourself...do you have enough knowledge of your business and industry?

Learn more

What trade journals are available to read?

What trade associations are you able to join? Do they offer educational programs?

What seminars, conferences and expositions can you attend to expand your knowledge and connections?

Do you have colleagues who may share their knowledge with you?

Consider joining an organization such as the National Association of Sales Professionals *http://www.nasp.com*

Share resources

Grasp the opportunity to serve your clients beyond simply selling them your products and services. Introduce them to new business opportunities and new vendors, who may help grow their company.

What resources do you have to share?

Examine your list of contacts.

Do you have a diverse network of clients and associates to share?

How much do you know about what they do?

Where can you meet more?

Visit networking events to meet more people.

    Chambers of Commerce
    Industry Associations
    Service Organizations

Volunteer with organizations that share your values and interests.

Make a note!

Make a note!

ENTHUSIASM

enjoyment • energy • excitement

Enthusiasm is a powerful characteristic that attracts people like bees to a honey pot. When we witness real enthusiasm in others, they seem to glow. They walk into a room and the room becomes brighter; when we engage in conversation with them, some of their enthusiasm seems to rub off on us, our spirits lift and our energy increases. It is very difficult to resist doing business with sales professionals who display enthusiasm for what they are doing, for what they are selling and for their clients.

♥

I love my life and I love my work. Neither are entirely perfect but I choose to focus on the parts of my life and work which I enjoy the most and I let my enjoyment show when I interact with everyone I meet.

When I focus on the more perfect parts of my life and my work, I become excited about the opportunities before me. I dream bigger and envision greater outcomes from my efforts and I cannot wait to get started on realizing my dreams...every task becomes a stepping stone to an outcome that I seek. My energy rises and my capacity to do my best work increases. My enjoyment increases and my work becomes such fun my biggest challenge is resisting it! I have to be reminded to stop working and take a break to refresh, recharge and renew!

My enthusiasm is contagious and makes it easy for clients to choose to do business with me. They enjoy having me around...I brighten their day and give them hope that they can enjoy the same excitement in their own professional lives. But they often don't realize from where my enthusiasm stems.

Source of enthusiasm

A large part of my enthusiasm comes from knowing how important my work is. At every stage of my career I realized that what I do is important; that I'm making a difference in the lives of others. Whether selling power tools or staffing services; security systems or quality assurance devices; computer training or sales training, I've always known that what I do helps others to complete a task or accomplish a goal that is important to them.

I'm not negotiating world peace or bringing an end to starvation and suffering, but every time I serve a customer or client, I know I make a difference. Every time I provide a product or service that fulfills a genuine need, I know I help someone move nearer to his or her goal.

One of the reasons I think selling is the best job on the planet is that no matter what we sell, no matter how ordinary or how extraordinary it is, we help others to complete a task or accomplish something that is important to them. Contrary to popular belief, sales professionals do not sell customers things they don't want or need. Customers are smarter than that; they generally make good-quality purchasing decisions based on the information provided by the sales professionals with whom they interact. Thus, whenever we sell something, we enable our clients to build their products, serve their customers or accomplish their task.

Whenever we make a sale, we help to secure the jobs of the people in our company or organization. Every time one of our customers or clients enjoys a success, we know we made a contribution to that success through the product or service we provided. Wow!

How can you not have tremendous enthusiasm for your work when you help so many people to accomplish so much? It's exciting to be able to make such a difference every day! It doesn't hurt either that successful sales professionals are well rewarded financially for the work they do.

> Along with enthusiasm come energy and a positive attitude. When I visit my clients and associates, they know that I will bounce into our meetings, greet them with a big smile and a warm handshake or even a hug if we know each other well. When they ask me how I am, I will say "Fabulous!" When they ask me what's going on, I share a success

> *that I or one of my clients is enjoying; I share the good news, not the bad, and create a positive environment in which it's fun and productive to do business together.*

Your clients are not served by hearing about the difficulties you face in your life and in your work. When you do talk about the down side of your work life, you should try to speak in terms that leave a positive impression. When you're tired from working too many hours, don't say "I am overworked" tell inquirers you are "Blessed with more opportunity than I ever dreamed of!" Sometimes you may share that you are "Quite amazed at how much work I can get done when I really need to!" When business is a little slow, they may very occasionally hear you say, "I'm so grateful for this quiet spell to help me refresh, recharge and renew!"

They don't need to hear about how tired you are, about the problems with the kids or the argument with the boss. It does not help them to have confidence in you if they hear more about your failures than your successes. When we talk less than enthusiastically to others, we process the message that this life isn't as much fun as it used to be. We create doubt among our clients and associates and we start to doubt our own ability to succeed. If we let our self-doubt show with clients, they will lose confidence in our ability to serve them and we may lose business. Once we lose business, we have confirmation of our inability to succeed and our self-doubt increases. Before we know it, we're on a downward spiral, from which it may be hard to unwind.

Almost all sales professionals hit a "bad patch" from time to time when sales are not where they should be. This doesn't mean we've completely lost our ability to sell; it means we have come up against some problem for which we are unprepared. Honest self-analysis will help us find the cause and fix it. We need to maintain our self-belief while we do so. Once that message "I can't do this anymore" gets out of the bottle, it can be really tough to put it back.

Maintaining enthusiasm

At the end of every work day I review the days' activities and accomplishments. I take time to identify the good thing that happened that made the day's effort worthwhile. Some days it's a very small thing and it's not always easy to spot. But everyday something good happens. It may be receiving a one-line thank you note. It may be a new contact. It may be accomplishing a less-than-favorite task. It may be closing a new piece of business. Every day something good happens.

Even in the "bad patches," if you focus on finding the good thing that happened every day, you will keep your enthusiasm high and pull out of the "bad patch" more quickly.

I used to work with a guy for whom "Every silver lining had a cloud!" He would always tell you why something couldn't be done. He would find a reason why nothing he did really mattered to anyone. Sometimes I was convinced that he considered his very existence to be irrelevant to anyone but himself. Being one of those people who are perpetually optimistic I found his attitude hard to deal with. Life seems so much harder for pessimists than optimists. Having to deal with all that doom and gloom, they have to climb so much further than the rest of us to reach the same peak.

Henry Ford said, "Obstacles are those frightful things you see when you take your eyes off your goal." Optimists stay focused, they face their share of obstacles and they face them with enthusiasm. They look for the opportunities the challenges present. They seek out the lesson from any failure. They keep their eyes on their goal and enthuse to all who will listen about their job, their products, their company, their clients and their life!

In my staffing days with Alfred Marks Recruitment we had a wall in the office where we pinned testimonials and thank you cards from grateful job seekers and employers. It was like a shrine. Whenever anyone on our team had a moment of doubt about their competence they would read a few of those notes and be revitalized. On another wall we had all the plaques commemorating the awards we had won for business success but those plaques never restored our confidence as much as that wall of client testimonials and thank you notes. I now keep my thank you notes and testimonials in a binder, which is always in my car when I'm out on business. If I get anxious about my ability to deal with a situation, I take a look, remind myself of past accomplishments and go forward with confidence. It's my proof book. I also use it to show prospective clients what has been written about me and about my business—the words of others are so much more believable than our own!

Create your own proof book: include thank you notes from people who have benefited from your energy, expertise and generosity. Use it to remind yourself and your clients how capable you are.

Enthusiasm for the products

When I began my sales career with Black & Decker, I had no particular interest in power tools. I had never used any. I didn't know what most of them were used for! I simply wanted to work for a company that would teach me to sell and reward me well for my efforts. Black & Decker did both.

As I gained experience, I gained enthusiasm for power tools or at least for what the power tools did for my customers. As I gained experience, I learned that it was the retailer who sold the power tools to consumers. My job was to show the retailer how selling Black & Decker power tools was a better proposition for his store than selling other products. It was my job to learn about what the retailer wanted to accomplish in his store and then to show him how my products would help him achieve it better than other products. I spent far more time talking about advertising campaigns and increased customer flow through the store than I did about drill bits and jigsaw blades, routers and workbenches.

When I worked with retailers who were excited about what they wished to accomplish in their store, I would become excited as well. I wanted to help them realize their goals. We would make plans for product demonstrations and special events, to attract more customers into the store to buy Black & Decker products and to see the broad range of other goods being offered. At the beginning of each new season I would visit every store and share information about new product introductions and the type of customers they were designed to attract. I would inform the retailers about the promotional activity that was to take place and what that could mean in terms of my retailer's accomplishing their goals.

In my role as a placement counselor and as branch manger at Alfred Marks Recruitment, it was easy to get enthusiastic about helping organizations find their new staff. You only need to hear thank you from one grateful job seeker to know that the work you are doing is powerfully important. You are literally changing lives.

In the staffing business, it was a blessing when talented job seekers came to you looking for help because they were unappreciated in their current job; were frustrated by lack of opportunity; or were excited by the adventure before them. We literally had the opportunity to make connections that set them on their life's path. Wow!

For six years I couldn't get enough of it. I watched people rise through the ranks in the companies I introduced them to. I watched companies I helped flourish in no small part due to the strengths of the staff my colleagues and I introduced to them. It was easy to be enthusiastic. It was easy to see that our work was important!

Often sales professionals tell me they find it hard to be enthusiastic about what they sell because their products or services are so ordinary; they are not glamorous or exciting but really quite mundane. I can understand that. There's nothing particularly glamorous about selling drills, lawnmowers or toasters. But when I think about the people who will use those products and the stores that will sell them the products become much more interesting. Most of the time, it's not about the product, it's about how the product will be used and the impact it will have on the life of the user.

Focus on what your products or services *do for people*, not what your products *do*. Think deeply about what you sell and how it impacts the life of the person or organization to which you sell it. If you are a car dealer, for instance, think less about the car and more about the journeys your customer will take in the car. If you sell clothes, think less about the clothing and more about the way the outfit will make your client feel when she's wearing it. If you're selling houses, think less about the house and more about the life that will be lived in the house.

If you're a banker selling loans, find out not just what your clients will do with the money you loan them but why they want the things the money will buy; what do they seek to accomplish? If you're selling education, find out why your clients need education; what will they do with what they learn? If you're in real estate selling office space, find out what your tenants do in their company and who their customers will be. When you know what your clients wish to accomplish, you can show them how your products or service can better help them accomplish their goal than those of your competitors.

As your clients strive toward their goals, you can support and encourage them and you can celebrate with them when they get there. You can tell the stories to anyone who will listen about what your products and services are enabling your clients to accomplish.

Most of us will probably never sell anything exciting and glamorous; most customer needs are fairly mundane by nature but the needs have to be met by someone. Better that someone be you or me than anyone else, right? Genuine enthusiasm for how your mundane products can help your clients accomplish their goals will eliminate your boredom and enable you to build stronger relationships, and have fun doing business with your clients.

Fascination

I am fascinated by other people's lives. They are so much more interesting to me than my own. I expect my life is fairly interesting to other people but not to me. I absolutely love my life but it doesn't fascinate me. I see my life every day; in fact I have no escape from it

ENTHUSIASM | 33

except when I'm focusing on someone else's. As I get to know them, I never cease to be amazed by my clients and what they do for a living; after all, most of them do something completely different than I do. Even those who are in sales practice it for different reasons. They are striving towards different goals than mine; they are trying to develop a life of their own that may be similar to mine but not the same as mine.

Most of us enjoy gossip. The whole basis of gossip is that the lives of others are much more interesting than our own. Often we pay far more attention to the goings on in the lives of complete strangers than the lives of those in our own household! As a sales professional, you can legitimize your curiosity about the lives of others by employing it to learn everything you can about your clients and using that information to empower you to provide solutions for their personal or business challenges.

The more you learn about your clients' lives, the more enthusiastic you will become about working with them. They all do what they do for reasons of their own. Some are pursuing dreams they've had since childhood. Others are just doing their best to pay the mortgage, put their kids through school or afford the price of pizza and beer at a ball game. Why they do the specific job they do is usually very personal. As Jimmy Stewart showed us in the classic movie *It's a Wonderful Life*, we don't always get to make our ideal career choices but that needn't stop us from having a wonderful career.

If you ever ask an entrepreneur how she got the idea for her business, sit back and prepare to take a book full of notes; she will tell you her story in some detail, with very little encouragement from you. Apart from the painfully self-conscious, most people like to talk about themselves and rarely get the chance. Ask some good open questions and give them the floor! Ask about the worst moments and you will learn about the creative mind and resolve she and her team bring to problem-solving. Ask about the vision, mission and future goals of the organization and she will explain why the work of her company is vitally important, her passion for her customers will pour forth and by the time you understand the goals toward which this leader strives, you will be almost as enthusiastic as she is.

The more you ask, the more you learn and the more enthusiastic you become. Not only do you build your own desire to serve the company but you also build a much stronger relationship with your business contacts because of the sincere and deep interest you take in the work they do. Once you become knowledgeable enough about your clients to be really enthusiastic about what they do, you then can help them grow their business in much more powerful ways than simply trading a product or service. You become a proactive supporter of their business and they begin to accept you as part of their team.

> By enthusiastically and proactively finding ways to help my clients, vendors and associates grow their businesses, my own business grows. When I did in-store demonstrations of Black & Decker products to help my retailers to promote their store and sell my products, their orders grew. When I spent time in store helping them create their displays, they expanded the size of the display and their orders grew. When I introduced new clients and vendors to the businesses I served in my Alfred Marks career, those businesses grew and came back to me to recruit the extra personnel they needed to manage their growth.
>
> As I enthusiastically demonstrate my commitment to their success by introducing my clients, vendors and associates to new business opportunities, they return that compliment by referring my services to others within their circle. And my business grows.

If you ever have to skimp on any aspect of doing your job as a sales professional, never skimp on enthusiasm!

♥

How will you unlock your enthusiasm?

Why is what you sell important?

Remind yourself every day how important your products and services are...you're changing peoples lives. Wow!

What do your products or services do for your clients?

What problems do your products or services help your clients solve?

What is the impact on your client's business (or life) of solving those problems?

How would your clients solve those problems without your products or services?

What is the "ripple effect" of solving those problems? (Think big...this question is the one that allows you to envision the most dramatic outcome of serving your clients!)

Develop new value proposition statements

Create statements that tell your clients what your products and services will do for them...not what your products or services do.

Create statements that include the outcome of using the product or service.

Create statements for every situation in which your products or services can be used.

Choose the most appropriate one according to the client you are addressing.

> ### Create a proof book
>
> Your "proof book" serves two purposes...it will remind you how good you are when you're suffering a moment of doubt and it will help to overcome client skepticism.
>
> Take a three-ring binder with transparent sheet protectors.
>
> Add thank you notes and e-mail messages, from colleagues, business associates and clients.
>
> Add client testimonials. (Whenever a client tells you he or she is pleased with what you do or have done for them, ask them for a written testamonial.)
>
> Add company newsletters and certificates of recognition, which inform about your personal successes.

Smile!

Research shows that sales professionals who smile a lot win more business than those who do not.

Make a note!

Make a note!

ACCOUNTABILITY

answerability • responsibility • liability

Accountability is often a much-underrated quality in a sales professional. Accountability means delivering on your promises. It means taking responsibility for your actions. It means answering for the consequences of your decisions. It means hitting your goals. It means honoring your commitments. It requires you to put all the pieces together to meet expectations. It requires you to ensure that all the tools are on hand to perform the task to the required standard. It requires you to engage all the resources that are necessary to accomplish the goal. It means adopting the attitude: "This is my job, my clients, my goals, my promises, my paycheck, my problem!"

Accountability is as vital as breathing in and out. It is essential to building trust with clients, colleagues, vendors and business associates. I worked on a consulting assignment with a client whose products are sold through independent sales representatives. These reps carry products from many manufacturers who all supply a similar target market. My client was having very erratic success among the group.

One day when we were discussing incentive programs to encourage and reward exceptional performance, she asked me, "Why should I have to pay extra to get them to do their job? Why do they take the job on if they're not going to do it? Why don't they just say no?" She is a very hard-working woman who was frustrated by the apparent lack of accountability of many of the reps. They didn't hit their goals and were full of excuses. She holds herself accountable to her commitments, her staff, her family and her supporters. It would never occur to her not to do what she was supposed to do: what she had committed to do. She simply could not understand why the sales professionals who had made commitments to her did not do the work necessary to accomplish the task!

♥

A sales professional is accountable for accomplishing the sales goals and for initiating and maintaining

ACCOUNTABILITY | 43

relationships with clients. Sales professionals are accountable for building the image and reputation of the company or organization with the clients they serve and for adherence to the rules and regulations that govern their industry.

They are also accountable to all the various stakeholders who have an investment in the outcome of their efforts: their dependents, their clients, their colleagues and stockholders. They are accountable to the vision and the mission of their organization. When in reality there is so much accountability, how is it that the popular image of the responsibilities of a sales professional is so different?

The image of sales professionals working flexible schedules, with no one checking up on them, is a very appealing one. The vision of limitless business lunches and exotic business trips, which are all play and no work, is a fabulous fantasy.

I cannot tell you how many times I've been told by unknowing individuals, "I'd love a job like yours: cruising about in a company car all day!", or "What a job! Staying in nice hotels at someone else's expense... you've got it made!"

Of course there are sales professionals who do enjoy luxurious life styles and lots of freedom of operation. There are sales professionals who work shorter-than-average-hours and make-larger-than average incomes. But they don't enjoy that lifestyle without a good reason! They have worked exceptionally hard to get to a position where their jobs *look* easy.

When the Williams sisters play tennis so athletically, we all think we could play. It *looks* so easy! When Brett Favre tosses a football up, we all think we could catch it. It *looks* so easy! When Tiger Woods sinks a birdie, we think the hardest part of his job is picking his outfit. It *looks* so easy!

It *looks* so easy because they have worked so hard to perfect their skills. They have practiced so much that doing what they do is as natural as breathing in and out. *It looks easy but it's far from effortless!* Top performers in any field work with mentors, coaches and skilled support staff to develop their natural talents to a level that distinguishes them from the pack. They practice, they perform and then they analyze the outcomes. They strive continuously to make tiny, almost imperceptible, changes that will give them an edge over other top performers. They decide on a change, they practice, they perform and they analyze again.

It *looks* so easy because they do it so well! The same is true of top performing sales professionals. They are so accomplished they make it look so easy! I had one sales coaching client who, when we were working on an exercise to develop new questions for her, practically yelled at me, "This is so easy for you!" I explained that I had twenty years of experience asking these types of questions: it's not easy; it's the extra practice that makes it seem simpler for me!

When we see a sales professional performing his or her job with consummate ease, we should caution ourselves against the thought, "Wow! That's easy; I wonder how I can get a job like that?" Rather we should be saying "Wow! How do I get to be that good at what I do?"; "How can I make my job *look* as easy as that?"

Training

Just like performers in any other competitive occupation, sales professionals needs to take their raw, natural ability and build on it with the right training and coaching. They need to analyze their processes on a regular basis. They need to make adjustments to their processes, heed the changing competition and try new strategies. They need to hone and shape their skills. They need to build on their strengths to reduce and eliminate the impact of their weaknesses.

It would be incredible to any of us, even those who don't care for sports, to hear a losing coach in the post-Superbowl press conference say, "Well, we did okay for a team that doesn't train!"

Taking classes, attending seminars, reading books and working with peers are all excellent ways of constantly reinforcing our basic skills. Practicing our presentations to ensure we're on top of our game can make all the difference to how we perform in front of the client. Reviewing what went well and what didn't go so well after our meetings and making changes next time is essential to growing our skills and our business.

> Even now, after over twenty years of selling, I still rehearse my meetings. I plan how I want each meeting to go and what I will do to take control from the beginning. I plan what I will do if the meeting starts to go in a different direction than the one I prefer. I rehearse my primary messages, so I am confident I will say the right things at the right times and in the right tone.

Fit to work

I don't know how many great talents have failed to reach their full potential because they didn't keep themselves physically fit or put in an amount of work equal to their ability. Maybe nobody knows. But it is a fact that even the best-trained professionals will struggle to achieve sustained success if they don't put in the necessary amount of work. If they don't discipline themselves to be at work, ready and capable to do their work, on a regular basis.

ACCOUNTABILITY | 47

Can you imagine Joe Torres, standing outside Yankee Stadium, saying to the fans after a terrible defeat, "Well, we were up all night playing cards. We were so tired, you're lucky we even came in to work today!"

Just like sports stars, sales professionals need to perform at an accomplished level on a regular basis to keep their jobs. They need to hold themselves accountable for ensuring that all the pieces are in place to do business when the opportunity arises. They need to hold themselves accountable for setting the scene for success.

We can only sell when our clients are available to us. In this increasingly over-scheduled world, getting appointments with buyers can be difficult even in the best relationships. It is essential that we keep the appointments we make.

While clients are understanding and considerate when we need to cancel an appointment for a legitimate reason such as poor health, an injury or an unreliable car, we cannot sell them anything if we're not there! They may understand but we still missed the order. While we may be able to rearrange the appointment and pick up the business later, we have lost time that could have been dedicated to winning more business. Of course there will be times when we are unavoidably prevented from performing our job but we should take all the steps we can to minimize those times.

Develop a healthy routine, which ensures good nutrition and the right amount of sleep. You need to be alert, enthusiastic and engaging in your client meetings. If you're falling asleep with exhaustion or are too ill to care, clients will notice and judge you, your company and your product by what they see!

Transportation is a vital element in our success, particularly in field sales. We need to properly maintain our vehicle so we can rely on it to work when we need it and, just in case the worst happens, we should always have jumper cables in our car. Even if we're in internal or retail sales, we have to be at work to serve our clients. Whether we use our own vehicle, public transportation or a car pool, we have to find the most reliable method available to us.

Think about the travel conditions. If you suffer snowy and icy winters in your sales territory, carry a shovel, a can of windshield de-icer and a bag of gravel in the back of the car. Allow plenty of time for the journey, drive safely and try to stay out of trouble. Check for road construction, so you can plan to leave earlier when necessary. And have food and drink in the car in case of traffic delays so you're in good shape when you finally arrive at your appointments!

These may seem like silly little details but it's our job to keep the appointments we make. It's our job to present an image of professionalism, reliability and commitment to our clients. It's our job to honor our clients by arriving on time, well prepared to do business. It's our job to secure the relationships and the orders that will generate the revenue that will pay the operating costs of our company or organization.

If we don't meet the clients because we don't take care of ourselves and our tools, we cannot build the **great sales relationships** that will bring us the orders we need to accomplish our goals. It's as simple as that!

Knowledge of your organization

As we discussed earlier, it is our job as sales professionals to know our business: to know our products, our policies and procedures, our vision, mission and goals; our company history; our industry history; our competitors; and where our industry is headed. And we must hold ourselves accountable for staying up to date in all these areas. Ignorance is no excuse under the law and it is no excuse in sales. It's our job to find out what's going on!

In an ideal world, we would be notified of changes that affect the way we do our jobs. The reality is that we are not always told. Life moves on at an amazing pace these days and it can be tough to keep up. But keep up we must if we are to enjoy rewards for the hard work we put in.

If you are a sole proprietor, selling then delivering a product or service, you are the person who designs the changes inside your company, so you are always aware of what's going on. In a small company, it should be reasonably easy to know what's going on internally, as lines of communication are often very direct and informal. In larger firms we rely on formal communication systems, with well-developed mechanisms for the distribution of important information.

In large and small organizations, sales professionals can be ill-informed about internal change, even with the best-designed communication systems, because some changes are perceived as having "nothing to do with sales."

The challenge for sales professionals is that we're not always around when new information is being distributed. We're often out in our territory working with our clients. Even when we work in internal and retail sales, we may be excluded from communication because folks simply don't realize we need to know everything!

So, how do we make sure we get all the news? We need to work closely with all of our colleagues and associates to ensure that we stay in the loop. We need to educate our colleagues and associates to realize that we need to know everything. I'm not talking about gossip here; I'm talking about changes in shipping and receiving that can affect the way our clients get served. I'm talking about changes in accounting and order processing. I'm talking about changes in vendors and carriers. I'm talking about changes in product specifications. I'm talking about anything and everything that may affect the way we deliver on our client's expectations.

It's our job to make sure that all the people we work with are aware of how important it is to us that we are kept informed about changes in their areas. It's our job to check in regularly and find out if anything has changed. It's our job to notify our colleagues, vendors and associates about changes in our area as soon as we become aware of them, as changes in the way we work may affect the way others need to support us. We need to receive information and we need to pass it along.

We must hold ourselves accountable for knowing everything: this is our job, our goals, our clients, our promises, our pay check. There is no one to blame but ourselves for not knowing what's going on. Make it a regular part of your interactions with colleagues and associates to ask about what's changing in their world and how those changes may affect your world.

Knowledge about your clients

As we need to know what's changing in our world, we need to know what's changing in our client's world too. Each time we interact with a client, be it a new client or an existing one, we need to build that knowledge. Just as your business may be experiencing change, so may be that of your clients. We must hold ourselves accountable for staying up to date with what's happening in our client's world and how any changes may affect us.

We need to know about takeovers and mergers, about new product lines and new markets. We need to know about the expansion, reduction or relocation of their workforce. We need to know about their internal re-structuring and changing policies and procedures. We need to know how they are performing against their budgets and sales projections. We need to know how these changes may affect their requirements for what we provide. Dig deep and explore what these changes may mean for your business. Your clients may not know how you can serve them as they move in a new direction. They may not have enough knowledge of your products and services to see how the change may increase or decrease their dependence on you. It's your job to learn everything and identify your connection to the new circumstances.

For some of us, change may bring new opportunities and for others, it may bring loss. Whichever it may mean to us, the sooner we know, the sooner we can start to address the consequences.

When your client's change could result in new opportunities for your products or services, you enjoy tremendous potential to strengthen your relationship.

Change is very stressful for most human beings. There is an entire industry built around helping professionals manage change. Having the support of a trusted partner in effecting change is very reassuring. Working with vendors you already know you can rely on is a great stress reliever. Helping your clients carry through the changes they seek to make by sharing your knowledge and expertise will show them that you are a trusted partner and a vendor they can rely on. If your client's change could result in a loss of opportunity, you need to start looking immediately for new business to replace it, either with that client or with others.

When you learn that your client is pulling out of a particular market you can ask, "So, who or what will replace you in that market?" If your client is planning to discontinue a product line, you can ask, "What will your clients use instead and from where would they purchase it?" Using that information you may be able to identify a new prospect for your business. You may be able to replace the lost business with new business from the company that will step into the gap left by your client.

Remember, it's not your client's job to inform you. It's your job to find out!

Knowledge of your industry

Do you know what your competitors are up to at the moment? Do you know what they're planning for next year? Do you know which of your competitors is calling on your clients right now, while you're sitting reading this book?

If your clients are worth having, your competitors will want them. Pay attention! Attend trade shows to see your competitors putting their best foot forward. Check out their web sites so you can see their information, pay particular attention to their news pages and testimonials. Know what they are saying about themselves. Know who else is talking about them and what is being said…you cannot know too much! Look for discontinued product announcements, new product launches and special deals.

Where you have close relationships with your clients, they may be willing to share some of what they hear from your competitors. I have benefited frequently from clients forwarding me the direct mail pieces they received from my competitors. Even if they don't want to go that far, you may still be able to learn from your clients by asking the right kind of questions. Questions such as, "What made you choose me instead of ABC Company?"; "Was there any part of ABC Company's solution that appealed to you?"; "How much more expensive were they?"; or "What is it about XYZ & Associates that makes you so loyal to us?"

Competition is healthy; it keeps us on our toes. Depending on your market position, you will get more or less competitor attention. If you are working for a market leader, everyone is after a piece of your business. If you are a sole proprietor or very small company, you often receive less attention. When I worked at Black & Decker and we had well over eighty percent of the domestic power tool market, we were everyone's target.

Stay in touch with issues affecting your industry. Keep up to date with regulations, research and trends. Is yours a growing sector or a declining one? Are there particular niches that offer more opportunity than others?

It's hard to imagine a banker not knowing what is happening with interest rates, a CPA who is unaware of modifications to tax laws, a car mechanic who doesn't know about the latest rules on emissions or a realtor who doesn't understand the implications of zoning changes.

Read the trade press. Join trade associations. Hold office in trade associations so you may shape the industry of which you are a part. If there are controversial issues affecting your industry, you need to be prepared for questions from your clients, vendors and associates.

It's your job to be in the know!

Knowledge – closing the deal

We must hold ourselves accountable for knowing what will make or break the deal with a client. We must ask the questions that enable us to package our proposition in terms that relate to our client's greatest needs and values.

If it's all about the price, we need to present our proposition with a pricing emphasis. If the client's biggest concern is post-installation technical support, we need to focus on that in our proposal and presentation. If the deciding factor is shared core values, we need to highlight the connection between our values and the client's.

As you ask your clients about their needs and the many different aspects of the proposition, ask them to prioritize the various factors in order of greatest importance. Make statements and ask questions such as "There are many factors that I need to consider in creating this proposal for you. It would be helpful to identify which are the most important to you. May we just run through the list and prioritize them?" Once you have that prioritized list, ask why each factor is that important.

I am frequently disappointed when I ask sales professionals, "What is the deal breaker?" and they reply, "I think it's this or that..." Don't think! *Know!* Ask the questions to find out. If the deal breaker is something you cannot provide then why waste time creating a proposal at all? You're wasting your time and your client's. That's not good for either of you and it's no way to build a relationship. If you cannot win the business because there is a requirement you cannot meet, you should discuss it and try to show the client how you offer other benefits that may be more advantageous to them. Or if there is no way to compensate with other benefits, you can bow out gracefully with your integrity and your relationship intact without investing any more of your time or energy.

Remember, it's your job to find out what your clients need. It's your job to understand why they need it. It's your job to provide a solution that meets their needs.

Being accountable is knowing you know, not thinking you know. And the only way to know is to ask.

Knowledge – understanding

In survey after survey, buyers complain that sales professionals don't ask enough questions. Instead of asking questions, they tell about what they offer and expect their clients to get it! Buyers also complain that those rare sales professionals who do ask questions often don't really listen to the answers, and wonder why the sales professional even bothered to ask.

There's no point in asking questions if you're not going to listen for the answers. Listening is a real skill to be practiced and exercised regularly. When you ask meaningful questions and listen completely to the answers, you will find your business will grow because you will offer solutions that more thoroughly meet your client's needs and they will say, "Yes, please" to you more often. So, what are meaningful questions and how do you learn to listen properly?

Meaningful questions are those that tell you not just what your clients need but what they will do with it. Why they need it and who will benefit from it. Why they need it when they need it. Why this product or service is important to the client's business. The more meaningful your questions, the more meaningful the answers. Asking well-thought-out, open questions (or probes) will show your clients you want to serve them thoroughly and enable you to get a more complete picture of the opportunity before you.

If you're a banker discussing a $30,000 loan, it would be obvious to ask what the money would be used for. If the answer is, "To build an addition to the house," you may consider that to be a better investment of $30,000 than if the money is wanted to buy a powerboat. However, when you learn that the powerboat is to enable the client's highly regarded, teenage son to compete internationally in high-stake races, your view may change. If the son succeeds, the financial rewards could be enormous! You may even wish to discuss potential sponsorship opportunities, as you envision your bank's logo on the winning boat in some major televised sporting event!

Dig deeper with your questions and listen completely to the answers. So, how do you listen completely?

We can listen to approximately three times as many words per minute as we can speak, which is why our minds can wander when we're in conversation. One of the most important things to do therefore is to curb our mind's wandering tendencies. When we ask questions that demand long responses, we can drift away, so ask short questions that beg fairly short answers. "Who will use the product?"; "What will they do with it?"; "How often will they use it?"; "Why would someone do that?"; "Why do your customers buy from you?"; or "Who else could they buy from?" If the answers you get are too short, you can always ask a follow-up question, such as "Tell me more about that."; "Please explain."; or "I'm sorry I didn't understand." (Yes, it's okay to admit you didn't understand—that way the client knows you truly want to understand.)

Focus your attention on your client. Look at him or her as you ask questions and as you receive responses. Concentrate on what is being said. Make notes and review what you heard after the client finishes speaking to clarify your understanding. Resist interrupting and let your client finish — you may think you know where her comments are headed but you could be wrong! Show your client that you are listening by nodding your head and making brief interjections such as, "Ah, huh," "Okay" and "Fine."

Here in the Midwest where I live, hunting is a major sport. Hunters are profound listeners. They learn to listen so completely that they can identify the movements of all the different creatures in the woods; they even know when a leaf is falling from a tree. They focus so intently on their environment they learn to shut out the noise of passing vehicles and farm machinery and are alert for the sounds of the creatures they seek. They recognize which noises to ignore and which deserve their attention. It's all about concentration.

As sales professionals, we need to listen like hunters. We need to recognize the sounds that tell us an opportunity stands before us. We need to learn to shut out all the extraneous distractions and to focus entirely on our agenda. By preparing in advance, creating an open and relaxed environment, asking meaningful questions and focusing our attention on the speaker, we can begin to listen more completely. By doing so, we will gain a deeper understanding of our clients' needs, create more suitable proposals and close more deals.

♥

How accountable are you?

Whether employed or self-employed, if you don't deliver the goods, you will ultimately lose your job.

Develop a system for reviewing your own performance

Are you making the number of client contacts you need to make to hit your goals?

Are you digging deep or simply scratching the surface when you gather information about your clients' needs?

Are you providing comprehensive solutions to your clients' needs or offering the minimum that will secure their commitment?

Do you do everything in your power to bring about the outcome you seek?

Do you ask management for assistance when you don't have everything you need to win the business?

Do you proactively build your knowledge or do you complain that no information is provided?

Do you ask for training or do you complain that it is never offered?

Do you develop strong personal links to colleagues and associates and create partnerships for winning and serving clients?

What is your share of the responsibility for failure?

What is your share of the responsibility for success?

Develop a maintenance schedule for all the tools you need

Car servicing and cleaning	Monthly?
Demonstration equipment	Monthly?
Cellular phone	Daily?
Computer, printer and accessories	Monthly?
Computer virus protection	Daily/weekly?
Computer password maintenance	Monthly/quarterly?
Application software licenses	Annually?

At the end of every client contact, take a few minutes to review what occurred and ask yourself, "What did I do well?" or "What could I have done better?"

After identifying what you did well, consider how you can incorporate that in future client contacts. After identifying what could have been better, make an action plan for how you will make the changes you deem necessary.

**Ensure you have all items needed
for your appointments:**

Notes from prior meetings

Proposal you plan to present

Contracts ready for signing

Calendar

Promised items from prior meetings

Order forms

Brochures, videos, specifications, price lists

Testimonials

Product samples

Product to be demonstrated

Make a note!

Make a note!

RESOLVE

determination • steadfastness • purposefulness

Resolve is imperative for anyone wishing to make a success of anything: it is especially important for someone wishing to make a career in sales. Selling is a profession in which there are many opportunities for failure, many barriers to meeting the goal. Sales professionals set themselves up for rejection over and over and over again. Without resolve, without determination, without a steadfast and purposeful commitment to accomplishing a goal, no sales professional should expect to achieve set goals and enjoy success!

Selling is not an easy job. It requires a combination of honor, enthusiasm, accountability, resolve and trust. It requires integrity, curiosity, passion, knowledge, imagination, creativity, commitment, focus, loyalty, respect and flexibility. It requires that every time we get knocked back, we dust ourselves off and get back into the fray.

♥

Selling is a much more complex job than many people realize, although the essence of trade is very simple. A trade is made when parties each find value in giving up something they own in exchange for something they wish to own. If what buyers need to relinquish has less value to them than the product or service to be received in exchange, they are happy to make the trade. If what sellers will receive has more value to them than what they will have to relinquish in exchange, they are happy to make the trade. Each party is content. It's a win-win situation.

Selling is made complex by elements such as competitive pressure and the need to generate profits. Corporations and consumers demand a choice of goods and services. Buyers expect to sift through a number of proposals before making a final decision about the solutions they select.

In order to ensure the honesty of their employees and officers, many organizations have rules in place that obligate them to obtain proposals from several sources before selecting a vendor, so friends cannot be favored with business to the detriment of the organization.

An increasing number of products and services are becoming commodities: price is the primary determinant. In such cases, the buyer's perception is that there is nothing to distinguish between the products or services and influence the buying decision except the price.

Quality, service, reliability, commitment and loyalty hold no value to such buyers. For them it's very simple: either your price is right or it isn't. If it is, you win. If it is not, nothing you can say or do will make a difference! But this is not true in all cases. In fact only a very small percentage of sales are determined by price alone.

The vast majority of buying decisions are based on the perceived value to the client of the product or service. Buyers want relationships they can commit to with vendors who will treat them with respect and loyalty. They want relationships with vendors who will honor their commitments and deliver on the expectations they have created. They are too busy to find new vendors every time they need to make a purchase.

As consumers, we get into the habit of shopping in our favorite stores because we know what to expect. It's not necessarily a perfect situation but it's reliable. The stores stock enough of what we know we like at prices we know we can afford to pay. The goods are of reasonable quality and the staff is pleasant to deal with. It's a hard habit to break.

In our professional lives, we get into the habit of buying from our favorite vendors because we know what to expect. When we need components to build the products that will keep our clients happy, we need to know who to call and when to expect delivery. When we need temporary staff to help us through a flu epidemic, we need to know the agency we call will send the right caliber of person with the necessary skills. When we call the office supply company, we need to know they will have the ink cartridges and three-ring binders we need to complete our presentations. They may not necessarily offer the best prices or the most choices, but we know what to expect. When we find vendors we can rely upon we resist making a change. It's a hard habit to break.

When prospective clients are loyal to their existing vendors it takes a lot of resolve, persistence and perseverance to convince them to transfer their business to you. You need to persuade them that the grass is truly greener on your side of the fence.

Attracting new clients

Clients who commit to loyal, long-term relationships with one vendor will transfer that loyalty to a new vendor, if they can be convinced that there is sufficient reason to make the switch. They are the hardest clients to win and, if you take good care of them, the hardest to lose.

These clients are happy with the products, the service, the quality and the terms of business from their current vendor. Buyers have little or no desire to mess with what is working: remember the adage, "If it's not broken, don't fix it"? Buyers have a mountain of work to do along with communicating and meeting with the reps from the companies from which they currently buy! Buyers have plenty to do without spending their time talking on the telephone with all the reps who would like to sell them something. They have too much to do to spend their time meeting a parade of well-dressed suits, all of whom offer essentially the same thing. To get on the agenda of these buyers takes commitment and persistence. If they are worth having as clients, they are worth working hard to win. It won't be easy but it should be worthwhile.

So, where do you start? As Julie Andrews told us in the movie *The Sound of Music:* "You start at the very beginning... it's a very good place to start!" Start with research to find out if this prospective client meets the profile of an ideal client, as defined in your marketing plan. Being a sales professional is like being a private investigator. We are constantly seeking out new snippets of information that will provide the insights we need to crack open our clients!

Start with the big picture, the easy-to-find information, the logistics. Who is the client? Where are they? What do they do? What industry are they in? Then start digging deeper. As we discussed earlier, we want to show each client we are particularly interested in them. Therefore, you need to dig deep enough to be able to personalize any contact you may have.

Check the prospects' web sites, look for stories about them in the news archives at the library; learn about their community affiliations and who their clients may be. If you're seeking business with major corporations, information is fairly easy to find. If you're selling to small businesses and sole proprietors, it's harder to get information for they hold their cards closer to their chest. It's harder but it's not impossible. It just takes a little more imagination, a little more creativity.

Often when we're selling to smaller companies, our reach is more local and our clients are in or near to our own community. We may have associates who know people from the companies we wish to get close to. We don't necessarily know everyone the people in our circle know, so ask! Ask your peers, your current clients, your vendors, your family and your friends.

If people you know have connections to a company you wish to approach, they may have useful information that could be beneficial to you. Ask them what they can share with you that may help you build your knowledge. Tell them why you wish to know, so they can choose whether or not to contribute. I'm not suggesting you ask your friends to share confidences with which they've been entrusted. Your friends and associates may be aware of accomplishments that the company is happy for anyone to know. They may know of particular challenges the company is facing, which may make it an ideal candidate for your products and services. They may have insight about the organization's everyday operations that they will gladly share. You may be astonished at the diversity and reach of your friends' connections and how much your friends know about them. You will be delighted at how willing they are to share that knowledge with you, when you ask.

Commit to the task

Once you have completed your initial research and determined that you definitely wish to pursue a relationship with the prospective client, you need to make a commitment that you are in this for the long haul! You are unlikely to make a couple of phone calls and win a client. You are unlikely to get orders by simply stopping by when you're in the area and asking to see a buyer on spec! It may take months, even years, to win new business: decide at the very beginning if you're willing to stay on task to the end. Steven Covey told us in *The Seven Habits of Highly Effective People* that we should "Start with the end in mind," and he's absolutely right. We should also start out knowing that this may not be a quick process.

I often compare selling to dating. It's all about building a relationship; only the purpose for the relationship is different. Most of us do not expect to marry the first man or woman we kiss. We don't expect to marry the first man or woman we date. Many of us wish to play the field for a while before settling down. With very rare exceptions, we don't decide on a lifetime of commitment after the first date. We take our time getting to know a potential partner. During each date we decide if we want to make another date. Sometimes we do and sometimes we don't. Sometimes one party does and the other does not.

As we become better acquainted with our dates we learn about their quirks and foibles. We learn about their values, dreams and integrity. We learn about their faith, politics and commitment. We learn to trust and sometimes to mistrust. We take our time and determine whether or not we wish to continue in the relationships. Some courtships last for years!

The same is true when developing new sales relationships. This is not a quick process. Resolve to commit to the process, no matter how long it takes. Remember you're trying to build a **great sales relationship**, not simply trying to pick up an order.

It will take both you and the prospect time to get to know one another. You may be ready to commit at the first meeting but your prospect may wish to play the field for a while before settling down. With very rare exceptions, buyers and sellers don't decide on a lifetime of commitment after the first meeting. We take our time getting to know a potential partner. During each phone call or meeting, we decide what the next step will be; whether or not there is any purpose in meeting again. Sometimes we want to meet again, sometimes we don't. Sometimes one party does and the other does not.

As we become better acquainted with our potential business partners we learn about their quirks and foibles. We learn about their vision, mission and goals. We learn about their policies and procedures. We learn about their expectations of vendors. We take our time and determine whether or not we wish to continue in the relationship. The purpose may be different from that of dating, but the process is very similar.

Persevere to the end

Put your whole HEART into building a new relationship and persevere to the end. When you begin your client development process you don't know what the outcome will be. You won't know for sure that you definitely want to win the client until you know her much better; but from the distance, she certainly looks like an attractive possibility!

As you commence your campaign to woo your prospective client, consider all that you have learned about the organization from your research and ask yourself two questions. First, why would this client benefit from a relationship with me and second, why would I benefit from a relationship with this client. If the client is to accept your invitation to a first meeting, he or she will want to know what the potential benefit is.

Share with the prospect what you have learned about his or her business. Explain how you have been of benefit to similar people or companies in the past. Tell your prospect exactly what the meeting will be about and how long it will last. Make it easy for your prospect to say yes by painting an interesting picture of the potential benefits of working together.

Much research has been done on the average number of contacts a sales professional has to make before getting a first order from a new customer. It varies between six and eight depending on what you read. There is a mass of similar research on the average number of contacts sales professionals actually make. It may not surprise you to know that overall the research shows that the majority of sales professionals give up after just one or two contacts. They demonstrate absolutely no commitment to winning new clients because they do not persevere in their efforts to make contacts. How can sales professionals expect to attract new clients if they don't stick with the process?

Seeking out new clients can be tough; rejection is not a fun part of life but finding new business is the key task of any successful sales professional. Companies relocate, merge with others and simply close down. Individuals change their careers, marry, divorce, retire and die. No matter how well we take care of them, there is no guarantee that our clients will be here forever. Circumstances well outside of our control are afoot to mess with our best-laid plans. We have to keep seeking out new opportunities to replace or enhance the business we are currently transacting.

Don't give up when your prospects say "No" the first few times you approach them. They are very busy people with pretty full schedules. Now you wish to add something else to their load. And the something you wish to add is something they don't think they need, as they are already well taken care of by someone else! Expect to earn your appointment in your prospects' calendar. Show your commitment to being of service by persevering in your efforts to arrange a meeting. Let them see that you firmly believe there is potential to do work together. Be creative in bringing your message to their attention. Stick at it and eventually they will give you a chance.

> It took six months before a retailer in Cheshire agreed to even talk to me about stocking power tools. It took fifteen months before a marketing consultant I met when planning my current business became my client. It took two years for me to get my first temporary workers on site at British Rail. But once I won their first piece of business, all three became regular clients.

I resolved to win their business and persevered to accomplish the outcome I sought. With each client, the approach was slightly different. Each needed different things from me along the way in order to build a relationship that eventually led to business. By sticking at it and being creative, I earned the breakthrough I needed and when I got my chance, I delivered on my promises.

Imagination and creativity

Think about it! Your prospects and clients are all individuals like you and me. They may work alone or they may be part of large or small organizations. They may answer only to themselves or they may answer to a supervisor, a project leader, a department head, a group of volunteers or a board of directors. When it comes right down to it, however, the deal is struck between you and your contact in the company. Others may need to approve the deal, but only you and the people with whom you interact as you put the deal together really make it happen.

Do all your contacts think the same way? Do they all support the same political party? Do they share the same faith? Do they have the same qualifications? Do they have the same values? Do they pursue the same vision, mission and goals? Do they get excited or upset by the same issues and outcomes? Do they use your products or services to solve the same problems? The chances are they do not. They may have many traits in common but they will likely differ just as much.

It makes sense then to consider the needs of each one independently and adjust your approach and style to meet that individual's needs. A statement that will enlighten one may confuse another. A promotional activity that will attract some clients may leave others cold. This is not easy.

As your relationship with your client deepens, identify his or her individual characteristics and seek to develop ways to connect on a more personal level. When you face challenges in moving the relationship along, think deeply about what you have learned about the client. Read and re-read your notes until you find the answers you seek.

Revisit the organization's web site. Pull articles from the relevant industry press and build your knowledge. When you face challenges in finding a connection between your client's problems and your products or services, think deeply about what you know about your business. Think about what the client uses to solve the problem now. What did the client use previously? Think about your other clients and the problems they have experienced. What solutions have you crafted for them? What outcomes did you deliver?

Sit down with your colleagues, share your challenges and pick their brains. Don't just ask other sales professionals for help; call on colleagues from several departments if you can. If you're a sole proprietor with no colleagues to call upon, ask other business associates whose judgment you trust. Develop a group of professionals, with different skills, experiences and perspectives on whom you may call for this purpose. Your colleagues or associates will be honored that you respect their professional judgment and they will be glad to offer their input, so long as you are not calling on them so frequently that they neglect their own tasks! Offer to reciprocate in similar fashion or find a way to reward them for their time.

Get as many ideas on the table as possible and consider the potential impact of each. Consider positive and negative consequences. Don't judge ideas as good or bad; judge them as different. Twenty years ago most of us would have judged it a ridiculous notion that we would carry a personal computer around in our backpack or briefcase…now we can carry one in our pocket!

Encourage people to share their craziest notions; sometimes those notions can be developed by the group and made to work!

Albert Einstein is often deemed to be one of the smartest people of the twentieth century. He frequently denied it, saying that he wasn't smarter than others; he simply stayed with the problems longer. If your prospective clients are worth winning, then overcoming the obstacles to winning them is worth you staying with the problems longer. Don't give up until you've exhausted the possibilities. If your clients are worth keeping and their problems are worth solving, stay with them longer; don't give up until you've explored all the options.

Resolve to find the answers to all the questions. Resolve to find the solutions to all the challenges. Draw on all your knowledge: your knowledge of your clients, of your company, of your products and services, of your industry and of your competitors. Put your imagination and creativity to work to overcome the challenges you face and you will win more customers and close more deals.

When you put a well-thought-out solution to their problems before your clients and prospects, share with them details of the steps and process you went through to craft it, they will be impressed by your resolve. They will recognize that you will go the extra mile to serve them when necessary and they will be honored by that.

When you finally come up with the great idea that unlocks your prospect's schedule and gets you that important first meeting, it will be worth the effort.

When as a result of that first meeting you go on to develop the relationship that generates the orders that make this your most profitable account, you will see just reward for sticking with the problems longer.

If it is true that "Most people give up just when they're about to achieve success. They quit on the one yard line. They give up at the last minute of the game one foot from a winning touch," as Ross Perot so unequivocally stated, then it stands to reason that those of us who resolve to keep going to the very end will win more often.

♥

How much resolve do you need?

How much work do you have to do before your prospects become clients? Which clients should you resolve to win?

Create a system for qualifying prospects

It is much easier to resolve to stay with the process if you know you're talking to the right prospects! Consider these criteria:

Demographic profile
commercial, residential
non-profit, government, institutions
market sector, location, size

Psychographic profile
values, opinions, culture

Expenditure budget
how much they spend
when they will buy

Buying cycle
how often they buy
potential for repeat business

> ### Review your sales process
>
> How do you identify your prospects?
>
> How do you make initial contact with them?
>
> How many contacts do you make before your first meeting?
>
> How many meetings before you provide a demonstration?
>
> How many meetings before you prepare a proposal?
>
> How many meetings after delivering the proposal before you get a decision?
>
> Are there certain categories of prospect that become clients more easily?
>
> It is much easier to resolve to stay with the process if you know how long it typically takes!

Build your brainstorming base

Who may be willing to share their ideas and creativity with you?

How will you repay them?

Will you meet as a team or separately?

Will you meet on an issue by issue basis or at regular intervals?

Will you ask for different help from members of the group?

How will you ensure diversity of thinking?

Are some issues best discussed in-house?

We must persevere to the end when pursuing business, which means recognizing when to quit. We must not quit too soon but there is no point continuing in a pursuit that will never bring reward. Review your sales performance to identify the typical elements of a winning negotiation. If you typically win business after ten interactions, it may be reasonable to assume that you are still in a winnable situation after eight interactions and unlikely to be in a winnable situation after twenty interactions. Compare your average sales performance with other sales professionals in your organization or industry to set some benchmarks. Never quit without asking buyers how they envision the negotiation concluding.

Develop criteria for knowing when to quit!

Are we moving forward in the process?	YES/NO
Is any new information being shared?	YES/NO
Does the client have a budget?	YES/NO
Does the client have a timeline?	YES/NO
Is the buyer committed to change vendors?	YES/NO

Make a note!

Make a note!

TRUST
integrity • reliability • faith

Trust is difficult to describe. Trust is a feeling; a sense; a state of knowing that this is a good person; a good decision: a good product. In its purest form trust is given freely to another person, without any prior evidence that the recipient will not abuse it.

Trust is fundamental to any meaningful relationship, personal or business. We need to be able to rely on the people who fulfill significant roles in our lives. The trust of another is one of the most complex things we receive. In order to receive trust, we first have to give it. In giving it, there is no guarantee that recipients will offer us their trust in return. Once we receive the trust of another, we cannot assume its continuance. We have to show by our actions that trust in us is well-placed.

This is particularly important for sales professionals. Sadly, almost everyone you ask will be able to tell you a horror story about how he or she was duped by a less-than-trustworthy sales professional. By someone who didn't put her HEART into her job. As sales professionals, we often have to start earning the trust of our clients from a negative position. Buyers are finding us guilty and we have to prove ourselves innocent.

♥

One definition of selling in *Webster's Collegiate Dictionary* is: "To dispose of or manage for profit instead of in accordance with conscience." This definition makes it easy to understand why buyers are wary of the statements sales professionals make. Potential buyers often believe that sales professionals will say almost anything to get a sale. So many of them have been exposed to sales professionals who live "down" to that expectation that even the most trustworthy of sales professionals must work particularly hard to win and keep the trust of their prospects and clients.

In order to build **great sales relationships**, we have to build a foundation of trust with clients, colleagues, vendors and associates. They need to be confident that they may rely on us to do what we are supposed to do, when we are supposed to do it. That what we say a product or service will do for them, is what it will truly do for them. That all the terms of the agreement will be met.

Integrity

I am often asked, "What's the most important quality in a sales professional?" My answer is always, "Integrity." This answer is usually unexpected because sales professionals are most often associated with qualities such as competitiveness, tenacity, persistence, motivation, assertiveness, communication skills, etc.

All of those qualities are important in sales professionals too, but for me, integrity is foremost because it's about the choices we make.

Integrity means honesty, reliability, truthfulness, uprightness, morality, fairness and decency. Integrity is evident when we choose to tell the whole truth even when the partial truth may serve us better. It is there when we choose to offer the true price even when we know the client is willing to pay more. Integrity is choosing to honor your commitments even when it means passing up a more profitable opportunity. Integrity is choosing to walk away from a sale because you risk a conflict of interest. Integrity is choosing to do the right thing.

My integrity was in evidence when I directed a new entrepreneur to take classes at the University of Wisconsin—Madison, rather than hiring me as his consultant and coach. The entrepreneur had been referred to me by his accountant for assistance a few weeks after launching his new company. I explained to him that for the cost of two hours of my time he could attend a program at the UW where he would receive eight two-and-a-half-hour workshops on the primary elements of business in which he needed to gain insight, each of which is presented by an expert from the community and that I am one of those experts. I pointed out that as a student of the UW program he would receive business counseling for free. He was so pleased we called up the UW and booked him into the course right there and then!

In sending him to class rather than engaging as his consultant, I showed the entrepreneur that his success was more important to me than getting his business. During that conversation I shared with him that I wanted him to use his time and money wisely, that it made sense to take the classes to learn some fundamentals and then, when he's ready to go to a deeper level, to come back to me. I was open and honest in my business practices; the entrepreneur learned that he could trust me to have his best interests at heart. My integrity was out in plain sight for him to see.

Why is integrity so fundamentally important in a sales professional? Simply because if we are to build **great sales relationships**, we need to build mutual trust. Without integrity, how can we build trust? If your clients cannot assume absolute honesty and fairness in their dealings with you, if they cannot be certain they can rely on you to do the right thing, how can you expect them to trust you? If they cannot assume absolute honesty, fairness and reliability in their dealings with you, why would they want to have a relationship with you?

If your clients do not care whether or not you have integrity, what does that say about their integrity? If they don't expect you to behave with integrity in your dealings with them, how can you expect integrity from them, in their dealings with you? If your clients have no integrity, why would you want to have a relationship with them? If they lack integrity, how can you give them your trust?

Whether self-employed or employed, we often experience periods of intense pressure to make sales when it can be challenging to our integrity.

If results have not been good for a while, we may be facing a situation where our job depends on getting some immediate results. Our supervisor may even have said, "I don't care what you have to do to get the business, just get the business!" It may be tempting to withhold information that would make our service less acceptable to the customer. It may be tempting to exaggerate the capabilities of the product. It may be tempting to fudge the terms of the leasing agreement.

You may try to create justification in your own mind for the choices you make. "My job depended on it. I had no choice."; "The boss doesn't care. She said so!";

"Once they take delivery, they'll love it so much, they won't care!"; "Everybody is doing it."; "That's how this industry works."; "You can't get business from that company any other way." or "No one will ever know."

When we're desperately trying to keep the wolf from the door, any business is good business, right? Wrong! Once we compromise our integrity, it can never be fully regained. When our clients learn we acted without integrity, the trust we worked so hard to win will be lost! Clients need to know they can trust us to do the right thing, whether they are watching or not. They need to have faith in us! Don't jeopardize your integrity, your reputation, or the trust of your clients and colleagues, to win a piece of business, no matter how much pressure you're under.

If your company's terms of business do not allow you to close an available deal because the client has a requirement you cannot meet, go to your boss and ask him or her to change or relax the terms in order to secure the deal. Try to negotiate with the client over the requirement that is causing the problem. Don't promise something you can't deliver. Don't make a commitment and then pray you get lucky. Engage the support of those who have the power to make the changes you need. If they agree, go and get the order. If they refuse, let the order go. Walk away from the deal with your reputation, integrity and conscience intact and keep the trust of your client and of your colleagues. Gaining one piece of business is not worth the loss of an entire relationship.

Don't kid yourself that "No one will ever know!" Someone will always know. Just like cheating at Solitaire, you will know!

The truth, the whole truth, and nothing but the truth

A golden rule of my professional life is "Never surprise the customers." That translates to "Make sure customers are always fully aware of the terms of the deals they are making—good and bad."

> I joined Alfred Marks Recruitment in 1987 and had six wonderful, very successful years in the staffing industry. I started as a counselor placing people into direct hire positions before becoming branch manager toward the end of my first year. With Alfred Marks at that time, if a client took on a new employee through direct hire, they were entitled to either a replacement if the new hire didn't work out in the first six weeks or a refund on a sliding scale if the new hire didn't work out in the first twenty weeks. These replacement and refund guarantees did not apply if the new hire was recruited via temp-to-hire. A temp-to-hire is like a long interview. By working together for a few weeks before hiring, both parties get a good look at each other, close up and personal. They each have all the information they could possibly need to make a good decision about working together. So the guarantees did not apply.

> One factor of Alfred Marks' offering that attracted employers to our company was the replacement and refund guarantees. It was imperative therefore when recommending the temp-to-hire option to clients that we ensured that they realized they would lose those guarantees. I would explain what a successful recruitment method temp-to-hire was; I would show them figures on the success rate, so they could see this was a very low-risk option. I helped them understand the terms, so they could make the best possible decision for their business.

It is far better to lose a piece of business because clients didn't like the terms of the contract than it is to lose clients because they found out the terms weren't what they expected and their trust in you was broken!

There will always be another piece of business, a second chance to prove your product or service and gain the customers' confidence but only if potential customers are open to doing business with you. Winston Churchill believed "Bad news travels around the world before good news has its pants on!" In these days of rapid transmission of information, news has never traveled faster. Switch on your TV, turn on the radio, pick up your newspaper, connect to the Internet; it's the bad news that receives most of the coverage; good news occasionally gets a short mention if the news channel is short of bad news that day!

If you or your company develops a bad reputation, you will be pushing up ever steeper hills to reach your goals.

Protect your reputation by being thorough in explaining all the terms of the deal, so clients can make the best choices for their businesses. When they really want what you're offering, as long as you can justify the terms of the contract, clients will accept your terms. Even if they don't accept the terms this time, the opportunity exists for you to go back again in the future. But if the client loses trust in you because you didn't explain the terms fully, all future opportunities are withdrawn!

Treat customers fairly

Treat all your customers fairly. Is it fair that the guy who negotiates better or demands more should get a better deal? Can you afford to change the terms of business every time someone pushes you for a better price, longer credit terms, higher performance specification or faster delivery times?

Let's assume your company has done extensive marketing research to establish the most likely customer for the product or service you supply. You have tested the product among the target customers to ensure proper fit for the purpose and aesthetic appeal. You have researched alternative products or services to understand what the differentiation needs to be and to learn how much customers are typically willing to invest. Your company has analyzed the cost of producing the product and the cost of bringing it to customers, which includes your salary, administration costs, advertising and promotional expenses: all the costs of doing and managing the business.

Your product managers have created terms of business, including price and credit terms, that they believe will provide exceptional value to the client, be competitive with the market and cover all the costs of doing and managing the business, while creating enough profits to satisfy the needs of shareholders and investors, as well as providing funds for future product development.

After all that work has been done, does it make any sense at all to vary the terms? Sometimes it does...*but not because we are being pushed by a tough negotiator.* It is common practice to offer clients better terms of business in exchange for bigger commitments.

We have different types and sizes of clients whose needs vary dramatically and it may well be appropriate to vary our terms according to the commitments of those clients. Having clients who sign long-term contracts, committing to buy a predetermined volume of product every month for twelve or twenty four months, provides us with the opportunity to accurately manage our inventory and control our expenses, which really enhances our cash flow and improves our profit margins. It is business almost every company strives to win.

For instance, I am sure there are many corporations across my community who use more office supplies in an hour than my company uses in a week or even a month! Those companies are unlikely to be paying the same price as me for their regular purchases. It costs less to sell $100,000 worth of product to one customer than it does to sell $10,000 worth of product to ten customers or $1,000 worth of product to one hundred customers. Passing on some of those savings is a great way of rewarding those clients who make bigger commitments.

Providing preferential terms to customers in exchange for bigger volumes or guarantees of future business is good business practice. It makes sense to all our clients, as long as it is done fairly and honestly. It does not make sense to any of our customers though, when terms are arbitrarily varied without a sound business justification. What fractures sales relationships is when clients discover that their vendors are giving better terms to other clients who do the same volume of business as they do!

Remember, trust will be given to you by your clients when they are confident that you will do the right thing, even when they are not looking. Treating your customers fairly is fundamental to gaining and retaining that trust. There may well be times in your career when your clients push you for some preferential treatment, so they may accomplish something important to them. As a sales professional, you are there to help your clients accomplish something that is important to them. If you can help them, you should. In considering your decision, however, give serious thought to the potential consequences. If you are confident that you can rationalize the deal to your other clients and colleagues, then do it. If you cannot rationalize it, don't do it.

Pricing is probably the most contentious issue you will have to address with clients. Quite naturally they all want the best possible price you can give them and you should never be offended when clients ask for discounts. You should always be consistent in applying your pricing structure, however. If you let a client have the ten unit price when they order five units, how much will they expect to pay when they actually order ten units? If you let them have free shipping this time, will they expect it every time? Be careful about varying your terms. Not only could it cost you the trust of some of your clients, it may also cost you a lot of your profits!

Say what you do and do what you say

One of the most powerful ways we gain and retain the trust of our clients is by keeping our word. Say what you will do and do it. Say when you will do it and do it at that time. I know that's just every day common sense, so I pose this question. If it's common sense, why do so many sales professionals not do it? Often, it's because they so want to meet the needs of their clients that they agree to everything that is asked of them, without first checking to make sure it's actually doable!

That is not smart! It is one certain way to ruin a sales relationship. If you over-promise and under-deliver, your clients will not care that you tried; they will care that you failed! As we talked about in "Accountability," you need to set the scene for success. One way you can do this is by checking that what you wish to do is actually doable. Your clients will respond positively when you say, "Ordinarily I would say yes but I know we're particularly busy at the moment. Let me check with Ted, the Production Director, and get back to you." or "A quick phone call to my boss will tell us if that's doable. Shall we try and get hold of him right now?"

Show your clients that you truly want to meet their needs and hit their deadlines by making sure that the promises you make will be kept.

Sales professionals are often accused of making too many assumptions. Yet, we have to make some assumptions in order to be efficient. If your advertised delivery promise is forty-eight hours from receipt of order, you have to assume that you will deliver in forty-eight hours when you discuss this with your clients. If you have a detailed specification for a product, you have to assume that the product delivered to your client will meet that specification. If you have outlined the way a service will be provided to your client, you have to assume that is exactly what your client will get.

You also need to check regularly to make sure those expectations are consistently being met; if they are not, you need to advise your customers accordingly. They may not like what you tell them but at least it will be reliable information.

> I once worked with an organization whose official policy stated that goods would be shipped two weeks from receipt of the client's official order. The sales staff faithfully promised to ship according to that policy every time they took an order. In reality, goods were shipped nearer to six weeks from receipt of the order! Client frustration was constantly high and the sales staff's morale constantly low. When I suggested they quote that shipping would be six weeks from receipt of the order they were concerned that the clients would not be willing to wait that long for their goods and therefore would not place the order. When I pointed out that the clients were already waiting six weeks, the penny started to drop. Clients weren't unhappy to wait…they were unhappy about being misled about the length of the wait! The source of frustration and mistrust was the unreliable shipping dates promised. As soon as they started telling their clients the true shipping schedules harmony was restored…it took a little longer to fully regain the trust!

Be precise in making commitments. I demand "precision speak" when agreeing commitments. When can I expect something to be delivered if I'm told it will be, "A couple of days"? When is "The beginning of next week"? Be very specific about the deadlines you agree to and then commit to them wholeheartedly. Shift heaven and earth if necessary to meet those deadlines. If you think you may miss it, tell the client before the deadline expires not afterward...once it expires and you haven't delivered on your promise, the client will tell you!

Clients know that stuff sometimes goes wrong. Totally unpredictable events occur that may push us off course. Clients want to work with vendors who minimize the impact of unpredictable events. They want to work with vendors who inform them early when unexpected challenges arise and then make every effort to overcome them.

If your clients experience a high frequency of broken promises, they will assume you are not trustworthy. They will cease to care what caused the promise to be broken: they will simply care that it was broken. Taking care of them well when an occasional challenge arises will build trust, as your clients see you working to solve the problems.

Supporters

As sales professionals, we have to trust that all of the people who contribute to what we do will play their part. We have to trust that our colleagues in marketing have done their homework and that customers really do want what marketing tells us they want. We have to trust the order processing department to input and expedite the orders we take accurately and in timely fashion. We have to trust the production department to build enough inventory to meet the requirements of our clients. We have to trust shipping to package the goods appropriately so they will be delivered complete and fit for their purpose.

Selling can be a very lonely job with long hours spent away from colleagues and away from the comforts of home. When we have a major success, there is no one there to celebrate with us. When we have a bad day, there is no one there to commiserate and comfort us. If we are to maintain our motivation it is essential that when we are out visiting clients and making commitments we are sure of our ground. That we know that the products we are describing are the same as those that production is building. We need to be able to quote honest shipping dates and firm prices. We need to be sure that what we tell the client will happen, will happen.

When we have absolute confidence in the people, systems and procedures back at base, we can go out and sell with confidence. We know we can answer any question the client throws our way because the information on which we are basing our answers is reliable.

Building great relationships with colleagues is one certain way to ensure their commitment to playing their part. Keeping colleagues informed of what is happening out in your territory is a great way of keeping them on your side. Let them know what's coming down the pipe. Let them know how important their part is to the success of the sales effort. Let them know how much you rely on them and how much you appreciate it when they come through for you. Say thank you!

None of us really wins alone. We all receive help from someone, even if it's only a kick in the pants every so often to get us fired up!

> I work alone in my business; I make my own sales and deliver programs I create myself. I have no colleagues or employees but I still receive a good deal of help. I get a huge number of referrals from associates that lead to business opportunities. My printer, graphic designer, and stationery store all come through with the goods when I need them. The reference librarian responds promptly to my research requests. My clients pay me on time. All of this help enables me to deliver on my promises. This help ensures that I meet the expectations of my clients and my clients trust and confidence in me grows. I make sure everyone that supports me knows how much I appreciate his or her commitment to me reaching my goals.

If you are part of a bigger team, make a point of thanking those people who contribute to your success. When you send a thank you note or e-mail to a colleague, copy her supervisor too. When you win an award, share it with all of the people who played a part. If you lead the team, hand out pay checks personally and thank your colleagues for their work, if you can. In doing so, help your colleagues realize the importance of their work and gain their loyalty.

"Thank you" is probably the most powerful expression in the English language. Use it sincerely and often, and you will earn yourself the loyalty of people who can truly empower your success.

> When I was fundraising for United Way of Dane County, I learned that one should thank donors seven times. I'm not sure that it's necessary to thank someone seven times for playing a part in our business lives but saying "thank you" at least once to a colleague every time he deserves it is a real loyalty builder.

Never forget that your client's trust in you is essential to building a ***great sales relationship***. The loyalty of your colleagues is crucial to you retaining your client's trust. If you are to deliver on all the promises you make to your clients, you need colleagues, vendors and associates who are loyal to you and as committed to doing their part as you are to doing yours!

♥

How will you display your trustworthiness?

What will you do every day that will earn you the trust of your clients?

Become expert in how your company or organization functions

Learn your organization's rules, so you know what you can promise

Learn about company policies and why they exist. If necessary obtain insight into how to explain to clients

Learn the procedures for getting tasks accomplished in timely order

Develop relationships with colleagues and department heads so you know whom to ask for help when needed

Pay attention to contractor services when appropriate

Become an expert in your products and services

Learn how to use the products and services you sell

Learn how competitor's products and services compare to yours

Learn the diversity of problems your products and services solve for clients

Learn the many ways in which clients use your products or services

How will you show that you deliver on clients' expectations?

Keep your appointments and honor your commitments

Don't agree to deadlines unless you're certain they can be met

Never exaggerate the capabilities of your products and services

Ask for the support of colleagues and associates, when necessary, before pledging to your clients

Confirm commitments in writing

How will you show appreciation to colleagues and associates?

Simply shake their hands and say "Thank you."

Send a thank you note and copy your colleague's supervisor

Share a prize when you win a sales contest

Give a personal gift for a significant effort

Refer business to associates who help you serve your clients

Share the limelight with those who assist you

How will you keep your supporters informed of developments?

Regular newsletter to highlight successes and challenges

Distribute a monthly internal report

Participate in company meetings and events

Share breakfast, lunch or coffee breaks to exchange news

Send e-mail updates during projects and a final report at the end

How will you ensure your supporters keep you informed?

Take them on the job with you, so they can see where they fit in your success

Check in with them, verbally or in e-mail, for updates in procedures and processes

Deliver on your promises and earn the respect and loyalty of your supporters

Share breakfast, lunch or coffee breaks to exchange news

As soon as you learn of a new procedure, honor your colleagues by using it

Make a note!

Make a note!

EPILOGUE

Hopefully you found *The Heart of Selling* an easy read with a clear and simple message.

Work to develop the skills, the knowledge and the expertise you need to honor your clients and all the people who contribute to you accomplishing your goals. The rewards will make the effort more than worthwhile.

Recognize and value the contribution that you and your products and services make to the lives of others. Your enthusiasm will grow and you will have more fun at work. You will be more effective when you enjoy your work more and the rewards will be greater.

Hold yourself accountable for accomplishing the task. If you do everything you can and engage everyone you need to meet your goal, you will need no excuses. You will hit your goals and meet expectations! And the rewards for your efforts will increase.

Steadfast and purposeful effort will take you where you have resolved to go…it may not be quick and it may not be easy but with commitment and determination you'll make it and the rewards will follow.

> In my quest for the perfect outfit for a special event I met a woman called Dawn, who works in Customer Service at the corporate Headquarters of Jones of New York. I found the outfit on the website of Jones of New York but was then unable to acquire it through any of their stores in Wisconsin. I called Jones of New York HQ and explained my predicament to Dawn, who despite the fact she's there to provide service to retailers not consumers, spent several hours tracking the outfit down to a Macy's store in New York City. She called me to say, "Jacqui, there's a lady called Pauline at this phone number, who has your outfit in her hand. She won't move from the 'phone until she's spoken with you."
>
> Dawn exemplified the very messages in this book...she honored me by recognizing how important it was for me to get the outfit. She was pleasant and enthusiastic in contacting me to keep me apprised of her progress. She held herself accountable for satisfying my needs even though that was not her role in the organization, and she resolved to find the outfit and didn't give up until she had done so. She gained my trust and secured my loyalty.

With honor, enthusiasm, accountability and resolve, like Dawn, you will earn the trust of clients, colleagues and associates. They will reward you with their friendship, their loyalty, their support and their business. They will honor you with their testimonials, their referrals and their trust.

… EPILOGUE | 115

Now...commit to putting your HEART into your selling and enjoy it!

♥

HONOR ROLL

This book would not exist at all if it were not for my good friend Ron Phelps, who first planted the seed of the idea two years ago. Ron is a consummate professional, committed networker and wonderful supporter of people in whom he believes; he proactively promotes them among his contacts and helps them to accomplish feats they never recognized they were capable of...like this book!

What can I say about Kira Henschel, my publisher and her team at Goblin Fern Press? Ron introduced me to Kira. If memory serves me correctly, he actually said, "Kira coaches people to write books. She can help anyone...even you!" After working with her, I know Ron was right. Kira had to struggle with my British English expressions and grammar and helped me make the book intelligible to an American readership. Not an easy task, as I rather like my British expressions and some of them I did not give up easily! Thank you, Kira, for your patience and understanding; you truly are a friend.

Before I started writing the book I chose five very important people to support me in the endeavor. I asked each of them if they would read my book and give me their candid feedback concerning the content and readability. Each of them is in sales in different environments. They are all people with whom I felt safe. People who I was confident I could trust to tell me if it sucked, without actually saying, "It sucks!" To each of these people I owe an enormous debt. Not least because they didn't think it sucked!

Karen Ostrov, Principal of Konect Consulting. Ken Schuster owner of Schuster Construction. Cathy Burkland, Sales Service Director with Madison Gas & Electric. Tom Dahl, Financial Planner with M & I Bank of Southern Wisconsin. Kevin Mahaney, Commercial Banker with Capitol Bank. To my readers...thank you for taking the time to read the unfinished material and for contributing to the development of this work. My biggest thanks though are for accepting the enormous trust I placed in you to be honest about my writing and my message.

I am blessed with many talented friends and three in particular have helped me bring this book to fruition. I am thrilled to honor them here. My delightful design duo of Melissa Carlson of Melissa Carlson Creative, who designed the book's jacket and Cricket Girvin Redman,

EPILOGUE

who designed the inside: thank you...you each did a great job! And my fabulous photographer, Shannon McMahan of Shannon McMahan Designer Portraits, who helped me overcome my camera shyness! I love the images you created for this book.

Last but never by any measure least, to my husband and dearest friend Robert. Wow! You never cease to amaze me. How you handled my single-minded focus on this project, without any jealousy or judgment, I will never know! Even as you are striving to build your own new business and bring it into reality, you allowed this year to be all about me and my book. I thank you with all my heart. I'm lucky to have you.

To all my friends, clients and business associates who have encouraged and supported me in the creation of this work, in all sincerity, thank you.

Jacqui

RESOURCES

There are many places to look for information to help you develop your network, build your skills and expand your creativity. Some of my favorites are listed here.

Networking

Most public libraries maintain directories of local groups and organizations. Look for a chapter to visit in your area.
- www.chamber-of-commerce.com
- www.rotaryintl.org
- www.optimists.org
- www.bpwusa.org
- www.bni.com

Personal development

National Association of Sales Professionals•www.nasp.com
Sakowski Consulting, LLC • www.sakowskiconsulting.com

Quotations

To inspire, to make you laugh or to underline a serious point!

The Forbes Book of Business Quotations: Ted Goodman
http://www.quotationspage.com

Books

Citizen Brand, by Mark Gobé

The Experience Economy, by B. Joseph Pine II and James H. Gilmore

Why People Buy Things They Don't Need, by Pamela N. Danziger

Built to Last, by James C. Collins and Jerry I. Porras

Journals

Sales & Marketing Management • www.salesandmarketing.com
Fast Company Magazine • www.fastcompany.com
Entrepreneur • www.entrepreneur.com
Business Week • www.businessweek.com

ABOUT THE AUTHOR

Whether selling power tools to small independent retailers for Black & Decker, managing a staffing agency for Alfred Marks Recruitment or quadrupling the sales of Robot (UK) Ltd, an electronic security distributor, Jacqui Sakowski believes that selling is the best job in the world! She enjoys a successful sales and sales management career that has spanned two decades and four continents. She has served clients in Africa, America, Australia, Europe, New Zealand, Scandinavia and the Middle East.

In 1998, marriage to her American husband Robert, transplanted her from the heart of rural England to Southeast Wisconsin. There she launched Sakowski Consulting, LLC in 2001, to share her skills and expertise with individuals and entrepreneurs throughout North America.

As a coach, trainer and consultant, she empowers sales professionals to reach new levels of accomplishment and gain more satisfaction from their work. As a guest instructor with the University of Wisconsin–Madison, School of Business and with Wisconsin Women's Business Initiative Corporation, she helps new entrepreneurs to develop the skills they need to shape their dream of business ownership into reality.

Sakowski Consulting, LLC is the sales improvement consulting, coaching and training organization, which focuses on the growth of small businesses.

The mission of Sakowski Consulting, LLC is simple. We help new and established small businesses to flourish by developing the skills of their sales staff and by improving how they manage their sales operations.

Coaching

Working one-on-one with individuals, Sakowski Consulting tailors coaching sessions to the very specific needs of the client, including:
- Sales Skills
- Performance Issues
- Sales Management

Training

Sakowski Consulting provides group training covering all aspects of selling.
- Secrets of Successful Selling
- Successful Sales Management

These are one day classes designed for groups of three to twenty. Developing new skills requires fresh thinking, so this session is interactive, including individual and group tasks.

Brown Bag Lunch Meetings

One hour Brown Bag Lunch Meetings are designed to bring focus to an important element of the sales function, with minimal disruption to the normal routine.

Custom Training Programs

Programs can be developed to meet the very specific needs of an individual or an organization.

Consulting

We provide expertise to address challenges and opportunities in relation to your sales operation. Assignments include but are not limited to:

- Creating management tools
- Performance metrics
- Interviewing potential new recruits
- Creating strategic sales plans
- Client surveys

Speaking

Jacqui Sakowski believes that if you pay attention as you go through life you cannot fail to learn! Through thought provoking, high-energy, presentations and amusing anecdotes she empowers her audiences to change how they think about the way they address work and life issues. She enables them to face the opportunities and challenges life brings them by recognizing their own inner resources.

Please visit *http://www.sakowskiconsulting.com* to learn more about Sakowski Consulting, LLC.